Making Presents

Penny King

CONTENTS

Carolrhoda Books, Inc./Minneapolis

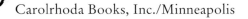

First things first

There is something special about homemade presents. The ten ideas in this book will make parents, grandparents, and friends very happy.

Staying safe

Before you start, here are some useful tips.

Some of the projects use materials that come with important instructions.

Ask a grown-up to read these to you, so that you know how to use the materials properly.

Always ask a grown-up to help with spray painting, working with acrylic, and baking.

Please help me

Spray painting
Always put things you want to spray in the bottom of a box. Stand back while spraying.

Drawing circles

The easiest way to draw circles is to draw around a cup or a plate, depending upon the size you want.

Cutting out

If you want to cut with sharp scissors, ask a grown-up to help you. Sit down to cut out. Make sure the sharp ends point away from you.

Wrapping presents

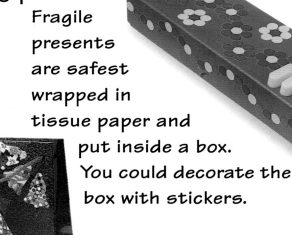

Fragile presents are safest wrapped in tissue paper and put inside a box. You could decorate the box with stickers.

Make your own wrapping paper by printing simple sponge shapes on brown or colored paper.

You might prefer to buy plain gift bags and decorate them yourself.

Mirror, mirror, on the wall...

Make this for someone special.

1 Cut out a rectangle of cardboard. Spray it gold all over.

Put a mirror in the center. Draw around it with a pencil. Then put the mirror aside.

2 Glue small odds and ends around the outline of the mirror.

All you need is ...

cardboard

pencil

little mirror

gold spray paint

glue

little toys

4

3 Spray everything gold.
Let the paint dry.

Glue the mirror in place.

dried pasta and pinecones

shiny bow and ribbons

5

Loving hearts

Give this to someone you love.

1 Pat some self-hardening clay into a fat pancake. Press the edges into a heart shape. Press a candle into the middle to make a hole.

2 When the clay has dried completely, paint it with red poster paint.

All you need is ...

self-hardening clay

3 While the paint is still wet, sprinkle glitter or sequins all over the heart. When the paint has dried, cover it with acrylic.

acrylic

paintbrush

candles

glitter or sequins

poster paints

7

Secret drawers

This is a useful present for very neat people.

1 Glue three large empty matchboxes together, one on top of the other. Cover the sides with wrapping paper.

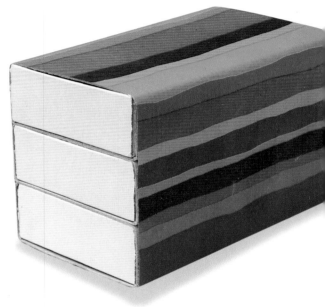

2 Paint the drawers, both inside and outside. Ask a grown-up to poke a hole in the center of one end of each drawer.

3 Find three buttons with a loop on the back. Push them through the holes. Slide a used match or a safety pin through each loop to hold the buttons in place.

All you need is ...

3 empty matchboxes

glue

scissors

paintbrush

poster paints

used matches or safety pins

3 buttons with loops

wrapping paper

9

Wild napkin rings

These are perfect for making a table look pretty.

1 Cut a strip of paper, about 7 by 2 inches. Bend it into a circle. Overlap the ends and glue them together.

2 Draw the outline of an animal on white paper. Color it with felt-tip pens. Cut it out.

All you need is ...

scissors

felt-tip pens

ruler

glue stick

acrylic

Paintbrush

construction paper

3 Glue the animal onto the ring.
When the glue is dry, cover
the whole napkin ring with acrylic.

Summer basket

These flowers will never need watering.

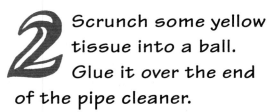

1 Cut a big and a small tissue paper circle. Put the small one on the big one. Poke a pipe cleaner through the middle of both circles. Bend over its tip.

2 Scrunch some yellow tissue into a ball. Glue it over the end of the pipe cleaner.

Gather the tissue circles around the yellow center and gently squeeze them. Unfold them.

All you need is ...

tissue paper

pipe cleaners

glue stick

pencil

scissors

basket

3 Push the flower stems through the holes in the bottom of a basket. Twist the stems to hold in place.

13

Party places

These funny faces show guests where to sit.

1 Roll some oven-bake clay between your palms to make a round, smooth ball.

2 Press the ball on a hard surface to flatten the bottom. Cut a deep, wide slit in the top.

All you need is ...

oven-bake clay

knife

poster board

felt-tip pens

3 Make eyes and a mouth from darker clay. Press them onto the face. Bake it in the oven according to the clay's directions.

Cut a small poster board rectangle and decorate the edges. Leave a space in the middle for a name.

Max

Jean

Anna

Valerie

Michael

Make a whole set of funny faces for your family.

Sponge jewels

These jewels are cheaper than diamonds, but just as eye-catching.

1 Cut lots of circles and triangles from different-colored flat sponges.

2 Arrange the shapes in a circle. Thread a large needle with a long piece of thin elastic. Push the needle through the top of each shape.

Leave a tail of elastic, like this, at both ends.

3 Knot the ends of elastic together to make a necklace.

All you need is ...

flat sponges

scissors

large needle

thin elastic

17

Book sssnake

A great present for bookworms.

1 Draw a wiggly snake on colored poster board. Cut it out. Draw around it and cut out a second snake. Set it aside.

2 Tear two paper eyes. Glue them onto the head of one of the snakes. Cut a ribbon tongue with a V-shape at one end. Glue this on the other side of the head.

All you need is ...

poster board

glue

old magazines

Pencil

Paintbrush

3 Tear little pieces from old magazines. Choose colors that will show up well on the snake's body. Glue them all over the snake. Add a torn paper mouth.

Finally, put some glue on the back of the snake's head and stick the head of the second snake firmly to it.

scissors

ribbon

19

Pot person

This funny flowerpot will make someone laugh.

1 Paint white eyes, pink cheeks, and a smiling mouth on one side of a clay flowerpot.

2 Add black eyebrows on the rim of the pot. Paint a pointed black nose.

All you need is ...

paintbrush

acrylic

poster paints

clay flowerpot

droopy plant

3 Paint black eyelashes, green eyes, and white teeth. When the paint is dry, cover the pot with acrylic.

Choose a plant with hanging leaves. Plant it in the pot and arrange the leaves around the face so that they look like hair.

Handy hanky

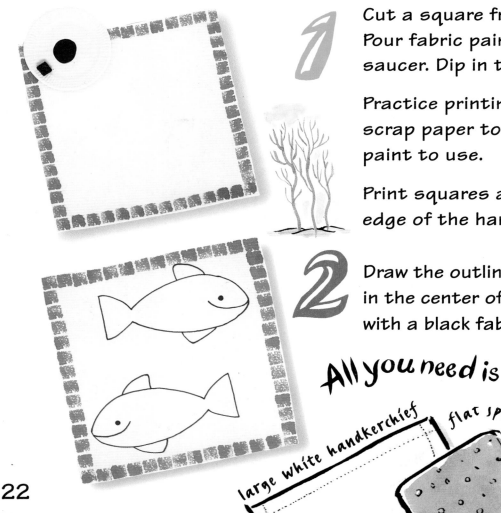

Wear an apron and roll up your sleeves for this project.

1 Cut a square from a sponge. Pour fabric paint into a saucer. Dip in the square.

Practice printing with it on scrap paper to see how much paint to use.

Print squares all around the edge of the hanky. Let it dry.

2 Draw the outline of two fish in the center of the hanky with a black fabric pen.

All you need is ...

large white handkerchief

flat sponge

fabric pen

3 Cut some more sponge squares — one for every color you want to use. Print one color at a time to give the fish overlapping scales. Print seaweed all around them.

apron

scissors

saucer

fabric paints

Index

Copyright © 1996 by HarperCollins Publishers Ltd
This edition first published in 1997 by Carolrhoda Books, Inc.
First published in England in 1996 by HarperCollins Publishers Ltd, London.
All rights to this edition reserved by Carolrhoda Books, Inc. No part of this book may be reproduced,
stored in a retrieval system, or transmitted in any form or by any means, electronic, mechanical, photocopying,
recording, or otherwise, without the prior written permission of Carolrhoda Books, Inc., except for the
inclusion of brief quotations in an acknowledged review.
Carolrhoda Books, Inc., c/o The Lerner Publishing Group
241 First Avenue North, Minneapolis, MN 55401 U.S.A.

Library of Congress Cataloging-in-Publication Data

King, Penny.
Making presents / Penny King ; illustrations by Mei Lim ;
photographs by Steve Shott.
p.   cm.
Includes index.
Summary: Gives instructions for making ten simple items that can
be given as presents, including a decorated mirror and candle holders.
ISBN 1-57505-206-7
1. Handicraft—Juvenile literature. 2. Gifts—Juvenile literature. [1. Handicraft.
2. Gifts.] I. Lim, Mei, ill. II. Shott, Stephen, ill. III. Title.
TT160.K475 1997
745.5—dc21   96-37356
Printed in Hong Kong
Bound in the United States of America
1 2 3 4 5 6 OS 02 01 00 99 98 97

DEMCO